M000073768

LIBRARY
FIRST ASSEMBLY OF GOD
1068 SEASHORE ROAD
CAPE MAY, NJ.

Presented to

_____

on the occasion of

_____

from

_____

date

_____

The Hound

of Heaven

A Contemporary Translation
of a
Timeless Masterpiece

by
Gordon MacDonald

Accompanied by
the Original English Text

by
Francis Thompson

VITAL ISSUES PRESS

Copyright © 1997
All rights reserved.
No part of this book may be reproduced
without permission from the publisher, except
by a reviewer who may quote brief passages in
a review; nor may any part of this book be
reproduced, stored in a retrieval system or
copied by mechanical photocopying, recording
or other means, without permission
from the publisher.

Original poem was published
in 1859.

Vital Issues Press
P.O. Box 53788
Lafayette, Louisiana 70505

Library of Congress Card
Catalog Number
96-61350
ISBN 1-56384-137-1

Printed in the U.S.A.

Contents

Acknowledgments

Research assistance to the author was provided by Judy Jacques.

Part I

Meet Francis Thompson

The next time you walk the streets of a big city and see a homeless man in a drugged stupor sprawled in a doorway, remember the name of Francis Thompson, the nineteenth-century poet who wrote *The Hound of Heaven*. The connection? Thompson, the man who wrote one of the best known pieces of religious poetry in the last hundred years, lived a not dissimilar homeless lifestyle for several years of his brief adult life. That a man, under circumstances such as these, could eventually leave a literary legacy of the quality of Thompson's is a remarkable story.

The Victorian era in England produced a school of remarkable poets: Byron, Shelley, Keats, Arnold, and Wordsworth, to name just a few. Their works are brilliant. But, it's probable that people of Christian faith are better acquainted with Thompson's *The Hound of Heaven* than any piece written by these men.

How *The Hound of Heaven* was birthed and brought to print is as modern a tale as any might imagine.

The only segment of Francis Thompson's life that came close to normalcy was his boyhood. Francis's father was a physician, and his medical practice was centered in the home where the Thompson family lived. The doctor and his wife, Mary, were deeply committed to Christian faith in the Roman Catholic tradition. Their devotion was a brave and perhaps lonely one since they lived in a predominately Protestant section of England, the town of Preston in Lancashire.

There were two daughters in the Thompson home, and then a boy, Francis, was born in December 1859.

The effect of Catholicism upon Francis Thompson's youth cannot be exaggerated. The priests of the parish were among the family's best friends, and regular church attendance was very much a part of Thompson's life. So dominant was this influence that Francis entered Catholic school at the age of eleven with every intention of becoming a priest. One imagines that his father and mother were inordinately proud of their son's intentions and would have been equally dismayed when, in his sixth year of study, school officials told them that Francis was being asked to leave. His "indolence" (we would call it laziness) made him incompatible, they said, with the kind of life demanded of a priest.

Only later would it become clear that Francis Thompson was anything but lazy.

Rather, his natural interest was in something other than theology. He was a voracious reader; he had the keen, analytical mind of a first-class thinker. But, at this age, there seemed to be no one who could encourage this strength.

The fact of the matter was that theology and the priesthood were not Francis Thompson's main preoccupation—a love for literature was. Before he was twenty years old, Francis had acquired an extensive knowledge of classical writing and poetry and was already making his initial attempts to express himself in written form.

Was the young man, now something of a failure at the age of eighteen, trying to please his father when he made a second attempt to train for a respectable career by entering medical school? If so, the sense of early failure was only compounded when, again, six years later, he failed a second time. He was twenty-four years old, with nothing to show in life except two long periods of education in which nothing worked. In a strange sort of way, the Thompson experience offers encouragement to young men and women who feel that they have tried hard and failed in their initial attempts to set a course in life.

It was during those years of medical training that something else attached itself to Thompson's life, and it never let go until the day he died twenty-eight years later. Francis Thompson became addicted to opium. We know it better today as a form of heroin.

The drug was known as laudanum in the England of those days, and it was widely prescribed by English physicians. People of great note—in the arts, the clergy, in public life—were well acquainted with laudanum. To some, laudanum seemed like a wonder drug, capable of masking every discomfort and pain (perhaps mental as well as physical), and, as a result, not a few carried some form of addiction to their grave.

These were days in which the dynamics of addiction were hardly explored or appreciated. Students of the life of Francis Thompson have speculated on the origin of his addiction, and some suggest it was a product of a serious illness he had in his twentieth year; others take note of the easy access he would have had to laudanum in his father's at-home medical practice. Then again, one of Thompson's earliest literary heroes, Thomas de Quincey, wrote a book entitled *Confessions of an Opium Eater,* which may have contributed to influencing the young man's choices.

Now in his mid-twenties, something of a disappointment to his father, and struggling with an entrenched chemical dependency, Francis Thompson chose the pattern of his literary mentor, de Quincey:

he left his family home and headed for London. He made his way to England's capital with little more than the clothes on his back. And, for the next three years, he learned about what we might call life on the bottom.

Francis kept himself alive by odd jobs, the sorts of things one got paid pennies for doing. At one point he was befriended by a prostitute who took him into her tiny apartment and supported him.

If there is a romantic angle to the story of Francis Thompson, it happens here. Throughout these years of struggle, the young man had made a consistent attempt to write, working mainly on poetry and a few essays. If anyone knew of these efforts or even read them, we are unaware of it. But, one day Francis bound a number of poems together with an essay and mailed it to Wilfrid Meynell, the editor of *Merry England,* a Catholic literary journal.

Something of Francis's sense of self-worth is revealed in the cover letter that accompanied the package.

> In enclosing the accompanying article for your inspection, I must ask pardon for the soiled state of the manuscript. It is due, not to slovenliness, but to the strange places and circumstances under which it has been written. . . . I enclose a stamped envelope for a reply; since I do not desire the return of the manuscript, regarding your judgment of its worthlessness as quite final.

The query letter was signed, "Yours with little hope." This was followed by a postscript: "Kindly address your rejection to the Charing Cross Post Office." Anyone who has tried to publish an article or a poem can identify with the pathos of Thompson's self-doubt.

When Thompson's package arrived at Meynell's desk, it consisted of little more than a sheaf of worn and dirty scraps of writing paper, the kind of unsightly mess an editor would be excused for ignoring. And, ignore it he did; Thompson's submission was set aside, unacknowledged and forgotten for months. Some might consider it a wonder that it wasn't simply thrown into the trash.

The result was predictable. Hearing nothing, Francis Thompson assumed the worst and drifted back into what can only be called a life of debauchery. However, the story does not end so sadly.

About six months later, something caused Wilfrid Meynell to retrieve the Thompson essay and poems and begin to read them. He was astonished at what he read: the brilliance of the essay, the quality of the poetry. Immediately he set out to locate Thompson and was, at first, unsuccessful. The poet seemed to have disappeared. Meynell made one more effort. He published some of Thompson's poems in *Merry England,* with the hope that the poet might see them and contact the publisher—and that is exactly what happened. Soon the two were in touch, and there began an association, a deep and personal friendship, that was to last for the remainder of Francis Thompson's life.

Credit Wilfrid Meynell and his wife, Alice, with discovering Francis Thompson, and for seeing that his God-given genius for writing would only be realized if he could break the bondage of his opium addiction. In such an effort, the Meynells sent Francis to a monastery in Storrington, where he attempted to break his habit. We would use the word *recovery* today in describing Thompson's rebirth into a better level of society. Soon he was writing essays, articles, and poems that attracted widespread attention.

It was toward the end of his stay at Storrington that Francis Thompson began to work on the poem *The Hound of Heaven*. No one who has studied it will disagree that the poem is clearly autobiographical or that only a man who had reached the lowest levels of life could have written with such passion about the love of God and all of its redeeming power. These lines were written by a man who had been reborn as it were, a man who had lost all hope and then regained it.

Until one has read *The Hound of Heaven* in its entirety and learned something of the mind and heart of the writer, it is tempting to be put off by the notion of God pictured as a baying dog crashing across the countryside in search of a fox or a hare. In truth, Francis Thompson probably saw many baying dogs during his stay at Storrington in the countryside.

Interestingly enough, the poem never mentions God as hound; only in the title is this done. But, a word picture of relentless pursuit is established in the title and never needs mentioning again.

The Hound of Heaven describes what many have experienced while working through the matter of faith in their personal lives. The notion that the love of God is the most important single truth a person can encounter comes hard for more than a few people. What Thompson points out in the process of his personal tale is that it is thoroughly natural for a person to fight off God's love with every ounce of effort he has. That was his experience, and he is blunt in describing it.

To capitulate to the love of God is to accept the fact that heaven has claims upon our lives: that we are accountable to the God who loves us for the way we live, the way we use what He has given us, and the way we intersect with other people and all of creation. This is no small matter, and it is tempting to seek alternatives if they are to be found. As the poet illustrates, most of us will seek every alternative to faith in God before we finally give in to the inevitable.

Francis Thompson begins his story with the words "I fled Him." That's the long and short of it all: I, Francis Thompson, used every ounce of energy to think and act in ways adverse to my Creator. I tried to find personal meaning, contentment, and satisfaction in nature and all of its beauty. I tried to find it in a pursuit of human perfection, which, if it is to be found, will likely be found in children (a Victorian ideal). I attempted to find some accommodation by bargaining with God. (It seems odd that many people feel they can do this. But, in one way or another, almost all of us make the attempt.)

As the race goes on, Thompson tells us, the eventual ending only becomes more inevitable. The footfalls of the pursuing God and the penetrating Voice keep getting closer, until Thompson is out of running room. He must surrender.

But, the surrender is not an easy one, as the poem makes clear. We are reading about the musings of what some might call a broken man—a man who looks back across the years and suddenly comprehends the wasted energies and motions, a man who comes to grips with how the best (and the worst) of intentions have gone awry. He mourns the bad choices, the unnecessary pain.

Must God always burn the wood and create charcoal before he can draw something of value? asks Thompson as he ponders the pain and the broken pieces of his own life. Finally, he hears those marvelous, reassuring words that all who have surrendered to God have heard in one way or another: "Come home; come home."

We live in a world in which many are running races similar to Francis Thompson's. All too often, many begin with the assumption that they can go it alone, that willpower, brains, connections, some enthusiasm, a few canny choices, and a little bit of luck are all one needs to establish an independent and free life. And, let's be frank: every once in a while, it does seem as if someone pulls this sort of thing off, that there are a few who manage to go to their grave singing Frank Sinatra's song "I Did It My Way." But, who can be sure?

Francis Thompson died in 1907. Attendance at his funeral was slim. The sum total of all his belongings could be put in a small cardboard box. He never did fully beat his addiction to opium. In the short thirteen years that spanned the bulk of his literary career, there were only a few periods of time when he was totally drug free.

One would wish that Thompson's story could end with a description of unlimited success—that all of his problems were solved, that he married, fathered children, and lived happily ever after. In a search for perfect endings, one would like to say that, in his final illness and at his funeral, an entire generation recognized his genius and good intentions and honored him in all possible ways.

But, they didn't—and he died in poverty and relative obscurity. His few personal friends were powerfully loyal. Beyond that, Francis Thompson never really received the acclaim that his work deserved until he was gone.

Speed-reading *The Hound of Heaven* will not work. The poem abounds with mystical reveries, an abundance of dreamlike visions and symbols. For the patient reader, the poem begins to disclose its secrets after many readings. Pay careful attention to the punctuation and note the words that are capitalized. They will assist you in knowing when Thompson is alluding to the Deity and when he is speaking of something less than divine. Meditate on the word pictures. They spring into life for one with a great imagination.

Daring to paraphrase this magnificent English work is a bit like serving a gourmet meal from the hand of a world-famous chef after one has brought it home in a doggy bag, frozen it, and reheated it in a microwave oven. The effort to paraphrase *The Hound of Heaven* was taken on in a moment of "craziness," but I have had no regrets. I used the exercise as part of my daily spiritual discipline, and I discovered something new about the love of God as I made my attempt to get into Francis Thompson's head and heart and deduce how he might express these thoughts were he speaking to an audience of people in our generation.

Francis Thompson has a lot to say to us. His life warns us that sometimes bad choices cannot be totally washed away when it comes to consequences, and that life is very, very tough for more than a few people. But, his story also affirms that even for those who suffer terribly, the love of God is real, assuring, and redeeming.

Today, he lives forever in the presence of the One who chased after him relentlessly until the race was ended. In the end, Francis Thompson came home.

Part II

The Hound of Heaven

A Contemporary Paraphrase

I fled Him, down the nights and down
    the days;
    I fled Him, down the arches of the years;
I fled Him, down the labyrinthine ways
    Of my own mind; and in the mist of tears
I hid from Him, and under running laughter.
            Up vistaed hopes, I sped;
            And shot, precipitated,
Adown Titanic glooms of chasmèd fears,
  From those strong Feet that followed,
    followed after.

            But with unhurrying chase,
            And unperturbèd pace,

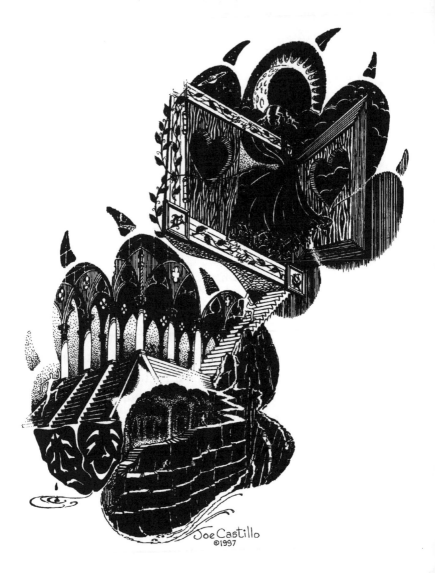

I fled Him, down the nights and down the days;
I fled Him, down the arches of the years;
I fled Him, down the labyrinthine ways
Of my own mind; and in the midst of tears . . .

Deliberate speed, majestic instancy,
>> They beat—and a Voice beat
>> More instant than the Feet—
"All things betray thee, who betrayest Me."

⬥

All my life—every day, every hour, throughout all the years—I have been on the run. My flight has been from One who has penetrated every dimension of my reality, even the nooks and crannies of my mind where I once assumed that all things could be logically figured out and brought under control.

Not only have I run, I have hidden from Him behind clouds of tears (in those moments when my heart was broken) and beneath the disguise of sustained hilarity (in other, rarer moments when it seemed as if life could not be better).

I have raced away from Him in moments of naive optimism, and, just as quickly, have dived for cover when life's circumstances unraveled and I was numb with fear. But, no matter my direction or my frantic pace, there has always been this relentless sense of pursuit, an awareness that there was One close behind who was not in a hurry, not upset, not panicked, and never undignified. Add to this pressure a Voice that is more present to me than even the footfalls of the One who chases, a Voice that says, "All of life will continually be unfaithful to you if you persist in being faithless to Me."

I pleaded, outlaw-wise,
By many a hearted casement, curtained red,
 Trellised with intertwining charities;
(For, though I knew His love Who followèd,
      Yet was I sore adread
Lest, having Him, I must have naught beside.)
But, if one little casement parted wide,
 The gust of his approach would clash it to.
 Fear wist not to evade as Love wist to pursue.

I attempted negotiation—as might an experienced felon—speaking from a heart that was willing to compromise ("How about a little of what You have to offer and a bit of what I might contribute?"). You see, I was terrified that, should I surrender to His love, I would lose my identity, my sense of personal freedom. I was aware that if I opened just one small window of my heart, the tornado-like force of His love would simply overwhelm me. Nothing in my fearful state of mind could conjure up an alternative that love could not overcome.

Across the margent of the world I fled,
  And troubled the gold gateways of the stars,
  Smiting for shelter on their clangèd bars;
      Fretted to dulcet jars
And silvern chatter the pale ports o' the moon.

I raced away—beyond the horizon, across the sky—in my frenzied frame of mind and irreverently, impatiently banged upon the gates of the heavens, seeking refuge from His pursuit. I badgered and cajoled, flattered and pestered any and everything that would listen.

⸻❧⸻

I said to dawn: Be sudden; to eve: Be soon—
  With thy young skyey blossoms heap me over
      From this tremendous Lover!
Float thy vague veil about me, lest He see!

⸻❧⸻

I cried to the dawn, "Come quickly,"
and to the evening, "Hurry up"; with your
shimmering beauty of gentle mists and
illusive shadows, cover me, hide me from
this overpowering Lover who pursues!
Blanket me with your splendor lest He
detect me.

I tempted all His servitors, but to find
My own betrayal in their constancy,
In faith to Him their fickleness to me,
  Their traitorous trueness, and their loyal deceit.

I sought to persuade all of His creation-servants to my cause but found them steadfast in purpose. Their fidelity to Him meant their disloyalty to me. If they would be true to Him, they would be untrue to me.

To all swift things for swiftness did I sue;
　　Clung to the whistling mane of every wind.
　　　　But whether they swept, smoothly fleet,
　　　　The long savannahs of the blue;
　　　　　　Or whether, Thunder-driven,
　　　　They clanged His chariot 'thwart a heaven,
Plashy with flying lightnings round the spurn
　　　　o' their feet:—
　　Fear wist not to evade as Love wist to pursue.

I searched for the fastest "horses" in all of creation, hoping to hang on for dear life to the mane of every streaking wind. But, wherever they blew, and however they blew—be it like strong summer breezes or the storm-forced gales—they drew His chariot through the sky instead of carrying me away. And, as they charged ahead, it was as if thunderbolts exploded when their hoofs struck the ground. It came to me again that the fear of Him within me could generate no scheme to outrace Him.

. . . Let me twine with your caresses,
Wantoning
With our Lady-Mother's vagrant tresses,
Banqueting
With her in her wind-walled palace, . . .

Still with unhurrying chase,
And unperturbèd pace,
Deliberate speed, majestic instancy,
Came on the following Feet,
And a Voice above their beat—
"Naught shelters thee, who wilt not
shelter Me."

So my pursuer persisted: never rushed or agitated, always steady, constantly in control. And, continually I heard the accompanying Voice that spoke above the sound of the footfalls, now saying, "There is nothing which will hide you . . . you who will not hide Me in your heart."

⟡

I sought no more that after which I strayed
     In face of man or maid;
But still within the little children's eyes
     Seems something, something that replies,
They at least are for me, surely for me!

⟡

I ceased searching for the epitome of
perfection in the company of men and
women. But, when I searched the eyes of
the children, I thought I saw something
in their innocence which suggested that
it is there that the "good life" is really to
be found.

❦

I turned me to them very wistfully;
But just as their young eyes grew sudden fair
With dawning answers there,
Their angel plucked them from me by the hair.

❦

I turned in their direction with hope that this might be my answer. But, just as my anticipation began to rise, just as I began to think that life's "good" might indeed be found in the beauty of the child, it was as if an angel appeared and abruptly (even angrily?) lifted them from my presence.

"Come then, ye other children, Nature's—share
With me" (said I) "your delicate fellowship;
    Let me greet you lip to lip,
    Let me twine with you caresses,
        Wantoning
    With our Lady-Mother's vagrant tresses,
        Banqueting
    With her in her wind-walled palace,
    Underneath her azured daïs,
    Quaffing, as your taintless way is,
        From a chalice
Lucent-weeping out of the dayspring."

Irritated at this loss, I thought of other "children"—the children of nature—who might offer a respite from the claims of my Pursuer. Thus I cried, "Open yourselves to me," to the sons and daughters of Nature. "Allow me entrance into your exquisite company. Let us become intimate as though embracing and kissing, not shackled with any cares. Let me be one with all of Nature as we eat and drink together (as if it were an event like the Sacrament) from the inexhaustible and magnificent resources of morning's delights."

So it was done:
I in their delicate fellowship was one—
Drew the bolt of Nature's secrecies.
    I knew all the swift importings
    On the wilful face of skies;
    I knew how the clouds arise,
    Spumèd of the wild sea-snortings;
        All that's born or dies
    Rose and drooped with; made them shapers
Of mine own moods, or wailful or divine—
    With them joyed and was bereaven.

My appeal seemed to be answered. Here I, a mortal, was embraced by Nature and permitted insight into those things most others do not see. As I pondered and studied, I thought I saw how things work in the skies. I reflected on how the clouds come into being as they are sneezed off the surface of the sea. As I viewed all this, I sensed how it shaped my own inner perspectives (my emotions, my moods), how the ups and downs of life seemed to find their origin here.

❦

I was heavy with the even,
When she lit her glimmering tapers
   Round the day's dead sanctities.
   I laughed in the morning's eyes.

❦

For example, I sensed an oppression, an inner gloom, when Nature signaled evening, much like one who lights the candles in the cathedral at dusk. Conversely, I felt the laughter of the heart when the morning came.

I triumphed and I saddened with all weather,
　　　Heaven and I wept together,
And its sweet tears were salt with mortal mine;
Against the red throb of its sunset-heart
　　　　　I laid my own to beat,
　　　　　And share commingling heat;
But not by that, by that, was eased my human
　　　smart.

I was up; I was down. I felt victorious; I felt blue in response to the unpredictable changes of the weather. It was as if heaven and I shared the same frame of mind—as if when we wept, our tears, whether sweet or bitter, were one and the same. When the heart of the sun beat, I could feel mine beating at a similar tempo. But not that, not even that, brought me wisdom or satisfaction.

In vain my tears were wet on Heaven's grey
  cheek.
For ah! we know not what each other says,
      These things and I; in sound *I* speak—
Their sound is but their stir, they speak by silences.
Nature, poor stepdame, cannot slake my drouth;
      Let her, if she would owe me,
Drop yon blue bosom-veil of sky, and show me
      The breasts o' her tenderness:
Never did any milk of hers once bless
      My thirsting mouth.

But, the fact of the matter is that we are strangers, Nature and me. My real tears fell upon an impersonal Nature. There was simply no response. In fact, we—Nature and myself—do not understand one another. When *I* speak, I speak words from the heart with feeling, with passion; but when Nature speaks, one hears merely noise, or one faces silence. My conclusion: Nature offers nothing which can satisfy the emptiness of my soul. I have challenged her as might a child: open your mothering breasts to me from the sky and draw me to you with infinite tenderness. Not once has she ever answered my challenge and slaked my thirst.

Nigh and nigh draws the chase,
 With unperturbèd pace,
Deliberate speed, majestic instancy,
 And past those noisèd Feet
 A Voice comes yet more fleet—
 "Lo! naught contents thee, who content'st
 not Me."

The chase continues, the Pursuer coming closer to the one pursued: never rushed or agitated, constantly in control. And, always the Voice—if anything, faster than the Feet—"Listen! Nothing will ever bring contentment to you; you who resist contenting Me."

Naked I wait Thy love's uplifted stroke!
My harness piece by piece Thou hast hewn
      from me,
         And smitten me to my knee;
         I am defenceless utterly.

I have been beaten, crushed in this unwinnable race. Deprived of all pride, pretense, and alternative, I finally speak (for the first time) words of capitulation to the One who chases. "I am stripped," I say, "of everything, and I await the force of Your mighty love. You have successfully chopped away at every scrap of my resistance; You have defeated me at every level. I no longer have any fight left in me."

I slept, methinks, and woke,
And, slowly gazing, find me stripped in sleep.
In the rash lustihead of my young powers,
        I shook the pillaring hours
And pulled my life upon me; grimed with smears,
I stand amid the dust o' the mounded years—
My mangled youth lies dead beneath the heap.
My days have crackled and gone up in smoke,
Have puffed and burst as sun-starts on a stream.

As I ponder the years of the chase, I feel as though I were in a delusionary sleep. Now as I slowly awake to new realities, here I am in this vulnerable position of surrender. Looking back to the misguided exuberance of my youthful years, I see that I cast off all restraint, and I alone created those conditions in which life simply caved in upon me. Now I stand amidst the rubble of all that's waste; my wrecked and wasted youth lies buried under it all. I have nothing to show for the days of my past; it is as if they have been consumed in fire and gone up in smoke, as if they are nothing but bubbles, which reflected the beauty of the sun, and then burst.

Yea, faileth now even dream
The dreamer, and the lute the lutanist;
Even the linked fantasies, in whose blossomy twist
I swung the earth a trinket at my wrist,
Are yielding; cords of all too weak account
For earth, with heavy griefs so overplussed.
Ah! is Thy love indeed
A weed, albeit an amaranthine weed,
Suffering no flowers except its own to mount?
Ah! must—
Designer infinite!—
Ah! must Thou char the wood ere Thou canst
limn with it?

Now it seems that all the reveries of this romanticist have failed. All the music of the lute player offers nothing. Even the wonders of making poetry—which once seemed to be so gratifying—is of no account. Reality is overwhelmed with sadness. Let me ask about the significance of this: is Your all-consuming love reminiscent of a weed—one which never dies—that allows nothing else, even flowers, to compete with it? Amazing! This must be so, Everlasting Creator. Amazing! You must burn the wood and make it into charcoal before you ever choose to do artistic things with it.

. . . I stand amid the dust o' the mounded years—
My mangled youth lies dead beneath the heap.
My days have crackled and gone up in smoke,
Have puffed and burst as sun-starts on a stream.

My freshness spent its wavering shower i' the dust;
And now my heart is as a broken fount,
Wherein tear-drippings stagnate, spilt down ever
    From the dank thoughts that shiver
Upon the sighful branches of my mind.
    Such is; what is to be?

Again, I scan the energetic years of my youth, concluding that those life-giving showers that might have moistened and brought a harvest to my life fell rather onto something like dust, and thus brought forth nothing of value. The gloomy state of my heart resembles a fountain clogged up with tears of depressing thoughts, which have fallen from my mind as dead leaves and twigs from a tree. That's the dreary sum of it all. What will come of all this?

The pulp so bitter, how shall taste the rind?
I dimly guess what Time in mists confounds;
Yet ever and anon a trumpet sounds
From the hid battlements of Eternity:
Those shaken mists a space unsettle, then
Round the half-glimpsèd turrets slowly wash
        again;
    But not ere him who summoneth
    I first have seen, enwound
With glooming robes purpureal, cypress-crowned;
His name I know, and what his trumpet saith.
Whether man's heart or life it be which yields
    Thee harvest, must Thy harvest fields
    Be dunged with rotten death?

When I muse upon the bitterness of my youthful life, my mind begins to wander toward the future and my aging years. It moves me to ponder the possibility that life can become even more grievous. Admittedly, it's difficult for me to imagine a "tomorrow," which time (like a cloud) so effectively conceals. But, every so often, in the midst of all this struggle, a strange and unusual moment occurs. It is as if a trumpet sounds from behind the walls of eternity, and the clouds momentarily seem to part, and I catch a glimpse of the Angel of Death. He wears the morbid robes, and on his head is the crown of doom. His name is not unknown to me; neither is his bugle-like call, which commands one's attention. In the moment of this vision, I cry out to You, O God: "If there is anything good that is to come out of my life, must it come only as a result of having been pressed with such ghastly misery?"

⸻❦⸻

Now of that long pursuit
Comes on at hand the bruit;
That Voice is round me like a bursting sea:
"And is thy earth so marred,
Shattered in shard on shard?

⸻❦⸻

The chase nears its conclusion, and an earsplitting noise like a roaring ocean engulfs me. Again, it is the Voice that I have heard so many times before, and now It asks, "Has your private world crumbled? Does it lie scattered in little pieces?"

"Lo, all things fly thee, for thou fliest Me!
    Strange, piteous, futile thing!
Wherefore should any set thee love apart?
Seeing none but I makes much of naught" (He
    said),
"And human love needs human meriting:
    How hast thou merited—
Of all man's clotted clay, the dingiest clot?
    Alack, thou knowest not
How little worthy of any love thou art!

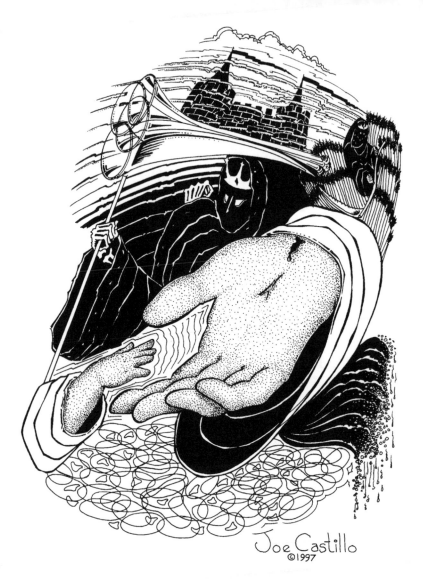

*'All which thy child's mistake
Fancies as lost, I have stored for thee at home:
Rise, clasp My hand, and come!'*

"Listen, everything that you thought might support your flight from Me flees instead away from you; it all deserts you. Why? Because you have fled from Me. Look at you, broken person that you are. Why would anyone find you lovable?" God asks and then answers, "None do. But I love you nonetheless . . . not because of what you are or because of what you have achieved. I simply love you. In contrast, the love of human beings is normally earned. How much of that love have you deserved? You, who may see yourself at this moment as the lowest of all human beings. You have no idea, do you, of how unworthy you are?"

"Whom wilt thou find to love ignoble thee,
      Save Me, save only Me?
All which I took from thee I did but take,
      Not for thy harms,
But just that thou might'st seek it in My arms.
      All which thy child's mistake
Fancies as lost, I have stored for thee at home:
      Rise, clasp My hand, and come."

"Who is there who will love you in all your brokenness? Only Me; only Me. Please understand that those things which I have denied you were not taken that you might suffer harm, but rather that you would one day seek these things from Me. As might a child in a moment of loss think that everything is gone forever, you are tempted to think that life is over. But, it is not. Everything awaits you *at home.* Arise, take My hand; *come home.*"

Halts by me that footfall:
Is my gloom, after all,
Shade of His hand, outstretched caressingly?
"Ah, fondest, blindest, weakest,
I am He Whom thou seekest!
Thou dravest love from thee, who dravest Me."

Now the One who was always pursuing from behind is alongside. The chase is ended. I sense a darkness. Is it danger? No, it is rather the shadow of His hand of affection reaching out to me. And, this One who has chased so relentlessly after me says, "You who were so foolish, so blind to the truth, so utterly weak: *I am the One whom you have always sought in all of your furious searches for security, well-being, and wholeness.* You find all you want and need when you walk with Me."

Is my gloom, after all,
Shade of His hand, outstretched caressingly?
'Ah, fondest, blindest, weakest,
I am He Whom thou seekest!'

Part III

The Hound of Heaven

Original English Text
by Francis Thompson

I fled Him, down the nights and down
   the days;
   I fled Him, down the arches of the years;
I fled Him, down the labyrinthine ways
   Of my own mind; and in the mist of tears
I hid from Him, and under running laughter.
      Up vistaed hopes, I sped;
      And shot, precipitated,
Adown Titanic glooms of chasmèd fears,
  From those strong Feet that followed,
    followed after.

      But with unhurrying chase,
      And unperturbèd pace,
Deliberate speed, majestic instancy,

They beat—and a Voice beat
More instant than the Feet—
"All things betray thee, who betrayest Me."

I pleaded, outlaw-wise,
By many a hearted casement, curtained red,
Trellised with intertwining charities;
(For, though I knew His love Who followèd,
Yet was I sore adread
Lest, having Him, I must have naught beside.)
But, if one little casement parted wide,
The gust of His approach would clash it to.
Fear wist not to evade as Love wist to pursue.
Across the margent of the world I fled,
And troubled the gold gateways of the stars,
Smiting for shelter on their clangèd bars;
Fretted to dulcet jars
And silvern chatter the pale ports o' the moon.
I said to dawn: Be sudden; to eve: Be soon—
With thy young skyey blossoms heap me over
From this tremendous Lover!
Float thy vague veil about me, lest He see!
I tempted all His servitors, but to find
My own betrayal in their constancy,
In faith to Him their fickleness to me,

Their traitorous trueness, and their loyal deceit.
To all swift things for swiftness did I sue;
Clung to the whistling mane of every wind.
But whether they swept, smoothly fleet,
The long savannahs of the blue;
Or whether, Thunder-driven,
They clanged His chariot 'thwart a heaven,
Plashy with flying lightnings round the spurn
o' their feet:—
Fear wist not to evade as Love wist to pursue.

Still with unhurrying chase,
And unperturbèd pace,
Deliberate speed, majestic instancy,
Came on the following Feet,
And a Voice above their beat—
"Naught shelters thee, who wilt not
shelter Me."

I sought no more that after which I strayed
In face of man or maid;
But still within the little children's eyes
Seems something, something that replies,
They at least are for me, surely for me!
I turned me to them very wistfully;

But just as their young eyes grew sudden fair
    With dawning answers there,
Their angel plucked them from me by the hair.
"Come then, ye other children, Nature's—share
With me" (said I) "your delicate fellowship;
    Let me greet you lip to lip,
    Let me twine with you caresses,
        Wantoning
    With our Lady-Mother's vagrant tresses,
        Banqueting
    With her in her wind-walled palace,
    Underneath her azured daïs,
    Quaffing, as your taintless way is,
        From a chalice
Lucent-weeping out of the dayspring."
        So it was done:
I in their delicate fellowship was one—
Drew the bolt of Nature's secrecies.
    I knew all the swift importings
    On the wilful face of skies;
    I knew how the clouds arise,
    Spumèd of the wild sea-snortings;
        All that's born or dies
    Rose and drooped with; made them shapers
Of mine own moods, or wailful or divine—
    With them joyed and was bereaven.

I was heavy with the even,
  When she lit her glimmering tapers
    Round the day's dead sanctities.
  I laughed in the morning's eyes.
I triumphed and I saddened with all weather,
    Heaven and I wept together,
And its sweet tears were salt with mortal mine;
Against the red throb of its sunset-heart
        I laid my own to beat,
        And share commingling heat;
But not by that, by that, was eased my human
        smart.
In vain my tears were wet on Heaven's grey
  cheek.
For ah! we know not what each other says,
    These things and I; in sound *I* speak—
Their sound is but their stir, they speak by silences.
Nature, poor stepdame, cannot slake my drouth;
    Let her, if she would owe me,
Drop yon blue bosom-veil of sky, and show me
    The breasts o' her tenderness:
Never did any milk of hers once bless
        My thirsting mouth.
        Nigh and nigh draws the chase,
          With unperturbèd pace,
        Deliberate speed, majestic instancy,

And past those noisèd Feet
A Voice comes yet more fleet—
"Lo! naught contents thee, who content'st
not Me."

Naked I wait Thy love's uplifted stroke!
My harness piece by piece Thou hast hewn
from me,
And smitten me to my knee;
I am defenceless utterly.
I slept, methinks, and woke,
And, slowly gazing, find me stripped in sleep.
In the rash lustihead of my young powers,
I shook the pillaring hours
And pulled my life upon me; grimed with smears,
I stand amid the dust o' the mounded years—
My mangled youth lies dead beneath the heap.
My days have crackled and gone up in smoke,
Have puffed and burst as sun-starts on a stream.
Yea, faileth now even dream
The dreamer, and the lute the lutanist;
Even the linked fantasies, in whose blossomy twist
I swung the earth a trinket at my wrist,
Are yielding; cords of all too weak account
For earth, with heavy griefs so overplussed.

Ah! is Thy love indeed
A weed, albeit an amaranthine weed,
Suffering no flowers except its own to mount?
          Ah! must—
          Designer infinite!—
Ah! must Thou char the wood ere Thou canst
          limn with it?
My freshness spent its wavering shower i' the dust;
And now my heart is as a broken fount,
Wherein tear-drippings stagnate, spilt down ever
     From the dank thoughts that shiver
Upon the sighful branches of my mind.
     Such is; what is to be?
The pulp so bitter, how shall taste the rind?
I dimly guess what Time in mists confounds;
Yet ever and anon a trumpet sounds
From the hid battlements of Eternity:
Those shaken mists a space unsettle, then
Round the half-glimpsèd turrets slowly wash
          again;
     But not ere him who summoneth
     I first have seen, enwound
With glooming robes purpureal, cypress-crowned;
His name I know, and what his trumpet saith.
Whether man's heart or life it be which yields

Thee harvest, must Thy harvest fields
Be dunged with rotten death?

Now of that long pursuit
Comes on at hand the bruit;
That Voice is round me like a bursting sea:
"And is thy earth so marred,
Shattered in shard on shard?
Lo, all things fly thee, for thou fliest Me!
Strange, piteous, futile thing!
Wherefore should any set thee love apart?
Seeing none but I makes much of naught" (He
said),
"And human love needs human meriting:
How hast thou merited—
Of all man's clotted clay the dingiest clot?
Alack, thou knowest not
How little worthy of any love thou art!
Whom wilt thou find to love ignoble thee,
Save Me, save only Me?
All which I took from thee I did but take,
Not for thy harms,
But just that thou might'st seek it in My arms.
All which thy child's mistake
Fancies as lost, I have stored for thee at home:
Rise, clasp My hand, and come."

Halts by me that footfall:
Is my gloom, after all,
Shade of His hand, outstretched caressingly?
"Ah, fondest, blindest, weakest,
I am He Whom thou seekest!
Thou dravest love from thee, who dravest Me."

I have this irresistible feeling that the Francis Thompson who strayed about on London streets, scrambled to make a penny or two in order to survive, and surrendered once and again to the seduction of drugs would have been unwelcomed in most churches, in most respectable communities, and in most of our lives. Yet, one cannot read this remarkable piece of poetry and not be impressed with the fact that beneath tattered clothes and untoward behavior lay a heart that was desperate to find order in life and peace with God.

Thompson's story and his great poem makes me ask these kinds of questions: *Have I passed a "Francis Thompson" on the street lately?* some man or woman whose outward appearance suggests emptiness, worthlessness? but, a person with a passionate desire to be made whole? who only needs a hand, a smile, a voice to point the way to God?

Another question: *is Thompson's description of the frantic flight from the "One who Pursues" a universal one?* In other words, have we all, at one time or another, been on a similar track? While perhaps not so dramatic, is there a popular tendency for all of us to try every available option in life before it becomes time to capitulate to the pursuing love of Thompson's God?

And, finally: *would a breathless Thompson, fresh from this race with God's love that he lost, attempt to persuade us that any attempt to elude the love of God—so powerfully passed to us through His Son, Jesus—is empty and absurd?* Was he trying to say that we might as well stop our own running and accept what God desires to give so graciously? My opinion? Yes! I think that's exactly what he's trying to do. Read the poem again. You'll hear him passing on to you the words he once heard: "come home!"

To order more great books from VITAL ISSUES PRESS, call toll-free 1-800-749-4009.

	DATE DUE	
9-3-98			

LIBRARY
FIRST ASSEMBLY OF GOD
1068 SEASHORE ROAD
CAPE MAY, N.J.